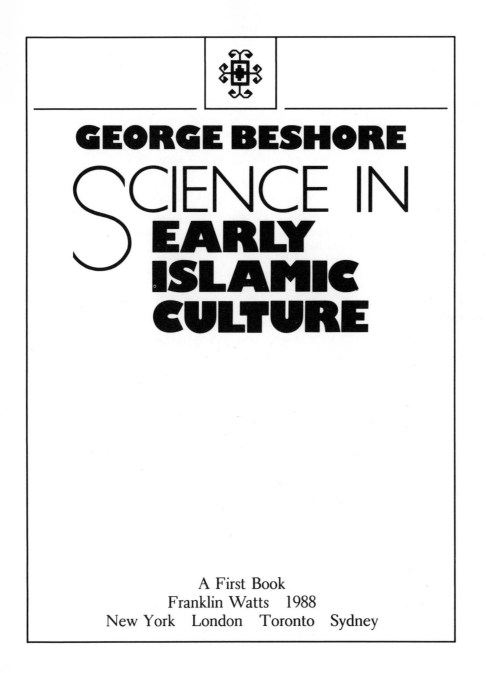

GEORGE BESHORE
SCIENCE IN EARLY ISLAMIC CULTURE

A First Book
Franklin Watts 1988
New York London Toronto Sydney

On the cover: A pump designed by Al-Jazari in the
thirteenth century. The geared mechanism draws water
from the tank through the pipe on the left.

Map by Vantage Art, Inc.

Illustrations by George W. Beshore

Photographs courtesy of: Fogg Art Museum: cover;
New York Public Library Picture Collection: pp. 11;
The Bettmann Archive, Inc.: pp. 13, 28, 47, 59;
British Library, London: p. 25; The Adler Planetarium:
p. 27; Art Resource/Giraudon: p. 30; New York Public
Library, Rare Book Division (Photo by Robert D. Rubic):
p. 35; Bodleian Library, Oxford: p. 44; National
Library of Medicine, Bethesda, Maryland: p. 52.

Library of Congress Cataloging-in-Publication Data

Beshore, George W.
Science in early Islamic culture/George Beshore.
p.   cm.—(A First book)
Bibliography: p.
Includes index.
Summary: Discusses the extraordinary scientific discoveries and
advancements in the Islamic world after the birth of Mohammed in 570
and their impact on Western civilization in subsequent centuries and
today.
ISBN 0-531-10596-2
1. Science—Islamic Empire—History—Juvenile literature.
2. Science, Ancient—Juvenile literature. 3. Islamic Empire—
History—622-661—Juvenile literature. 4. Islam—History—Juvenile
literature. [1. Science—Islamic Empire—History. 2. Science,
Ancient. 3. Islamic Empire—History—622-661.] I. Title.
Q127.I74B47   1988
509.17′671—dc19   88-2660   CIP   AC

to Margaret

CONTENTS

SCIENCE IN EARLY ISLAMIC CULTURE

THE ISLAMIC WORLD
c. 1048–1131 A.D.

RUSSIA

CHINA

GERMANY

FRANCE

HUNGARY

Vienna

Buda

Danube R.

BLACK SEA

ITALY

Palermo

Tunis

Tripoli

CRETE

CYPRUS

MEDITERRANEAN SEA

SPAIN

Morocco

AFRICA

EGYPT

Cairo

Jerusalem

SYRIA

Tigris R.

Euphrates R.

CASPIAN SEA

Syr Darya

Amu Darya (Oxus R.)

Samarkand

Nishapur

PERSIA (Iran)

Isfahen

Shiraz

Baghdad

IRAQ

Basra

PERSIAN GULF

Medina

Mecca

RED SEA

ARABIA

Nile R.

Indus R.

Delhi

Ganges R.

INDIA

ARABIAN SEA

Islam

Seljuk empire

Ottoman empire

A NEW ERA
IN SCIENCE

The future of science in the Western world looked dim as the sixth century A.D. drew to a close. People seemed to have lost interest in searching for knowledge about the nature of the world around them, which is the main purpose of science.

It seemed questionable whether civilization itself could long endure. The great Greek and Egyptian cultures lay in ruins. Rome, the last bastion of learning in the West, had fallen to the barbarians from Northern Europe in 476 A.D. Throughout the Western world the lamp of enlightenment was flickering dangerously. It seemed possible that its glow might be snuffed out forever.

This situation would soon be changed by events occurring far from the ancient centers of power in Greece and Rome. About 570 A.D. (the exact date is unknown) a child named Mohammed was born in the town of Mecca in Arabia. No one could foresee that this boy, whose parents died by the time he was six years old, would become the leader of a movement that would conquer the ancient empires of Persia and Egypt and spread its domination all the way from India to the Atlantic Ocean.

Wherever they went, Mohammed's followers would collect and preserve the science of ancient civilizations. They would also build new centers of learning and add many ideas of their own about mathematics, medicine, astronomy, and physics. Equally important would be their new approach to science. It used experimentation, observation, and careful measurement of natural phenomena. This approach replaced older methods of speculating about the nature of things, and it gave future generations the great legacy that is the scientific heritage of Islam.

MOHAMMED'S VISION

The new movement began about 610 A.D. (the exact date is uncertain), when Mohammed had a vision in a cave near Mecca. An angel seemed to appear, telling him to go out and found a new religion that would unite all of the people in the world under one God, with Mohammed as His major prophet. Science and learning were to be an important part of this new way of life.

Mohammed began to preach in the markets of Arabia, and the people rallied around him. They formed armies that swept north and captured Jerusalem in the year 637. Turning east, they conquered areas once ruled by the Babylonians and Persians. Continuing east, they overran central Asia, and in 712 they captured the ancient city of Samarkand on the main trade route to China.

At the same time, Moslem armies in the west conquered Egypt and the rest of North Africa. In 711 they crossed the Straits of Gibraltar into Spain. Moving rapidly north, within a few years they crossed the Pyrenees Mountains into France. For a time it looked as though they would conquer all of Europe. However, in the year 732 a Christian force defeated them near Tours, a city in France south of Paris, and Europe was saved from Moslem domination.

Mohammed (faceless and engulfed
in flames) and some of his followers

EMPHASIS ON LEARNING

Within a century after the Prophet's death in 632, followers of Mohammed's teachings ruled a vast empire that stretched one-fourth of the way around the world, from the Atlantic Ocean in the west to India in the east. These followers were (and still are) called **Moslems.** Their religion is called **Islam,** an Arabic word that means "submission to God." It is called Islam because Moslems believe that each individual must surrender to the will of God, whom they call **Allah,** to find inner peace.

Throughout this huge area the Moslems set up great centers of learning and collected all of the information they could find about science in the lands they conquered. The urge to do this came from Mohammed himself, because the Prophet taught his followers to seek knowledge wherever they went. Look for learning, he told them, even if this search takes you as far afield as China, the most distant place that anyone could imagine in those days. "He who travels in search of knowledge travels along Allah's path to paradise," the Prophet added.

The people whom the Moslems conquered were taught Arabic so they could read the Koran, Islam's sacred book. Otherwise, they were allowed to go on living much as they had when the conquerors came—as long as they submitted to Islamic rule.

The Moslems were curious about the natural world and showed great tolerance toward the scientific ideas existing in the lands they conquered. From the Greeks and Egyptians they learned about medicine and mathematics. The ancient Persians and the people of India had accumulated much information about the stars and planets. Engineering skills existed in both Egypt and the area along the Tigris and Euphrates rivers, where people had built great irrigation systems since ancient times.

In the northern part of what is now Syria, Moslem scholars learned of strange-looking numbers that had come from far-off

The city of Morocco

India. These numbers contained nine symbols that could be used to write any figure, no matter how large. The introduction to the West of these Indian numbers was one of the earliest of many important contributions to science that would come from the world of Islam.

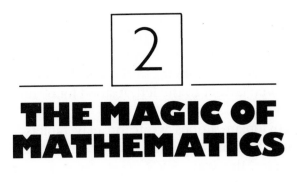

THE MAGIC OF MATHEMATICS

When the Moslem armies reached Syria in the seventh century, they found a Christian bishop named Severus Sebokht writing about numbers familiar to everyone today. They are called Arabic numerals, but the Arabs did not invent them. These symbols originated centuries earlier far to the east. They got their name because the Arabs adopted this system and spread it throughout the Western world.

MANY NUMBER SYSTEMS

People in the West had used many different numerical systems. Few were very good by modern standards. The Greeks, who had been leaders in spreading their civilization throughout the Mediterranean area, used letters from their alphabet to stand for numbers. The Romans, who had conquered the entire Western world as it was known to them, had a clumsy system that used an I for one, a V for five, an X for ten, and so on.

One of the best of the ancient systems was also the oldest. It had been developed in the third millennium B.C. by the Babylonians. They assigned different values to symbols according to where they appear from left to right, as we do in modern mathematics. A 1 on the right would equal one unit. The same symbol, when moved over one column to the left, became a 10. When it was moved even farther to the left, it stood for 60 (instead of 100 as it does today).

The Babylonian scribes wrote on clay tablets, using wedge-shaped marks to represent numbers. The number 1 was written like this: 𐎚 ; a 5 this way: 𐎚𐎚𐎚 𐎚𐎚

Tens were made by modifying and turning the wedges on their sides, like this: ◀

The number 22 was written: ◀
(Two 10s and two units) ◀ 𐎚𐎚

55 was written: ◀◀ 𐎚𐎚𐎚
(Five 10s and five units) ◀◀ 𐎚𐎚 ◀

When writing larger numbers, the Babylonians used multiples of 60 plus 10s and units. Three hundred was written: 𐎚𐎚𐎚 𐎚𐎚 (five 60s).

Four hundred was 𐎚𐎚𐎚 ◀◀ (six 60s plus four 10s). 𐎚𐎚𐎚 ◀◀

The figure 442 (seven 60s, two 10s, and two units) was ▷ 𐎚𐎚𐎚𐎚 𐎚𐎚 ▷ 𐎚𐎚𐎚

Early forms of the Babylonian system did not have a symbol for our zero. Hence, people were sometimes confused about whether a number stood for units, 10s, or 60s. If a scribe was careless, a number such as 180 (𒌋𒌋𒌋 = three 60s) might be mistakenly read as 3 (three units). About the fourth century B.C. the Babylonians corrected this problem by adopting a symbol that stood for the modern zero.

The use of nine symbols to write any figure, and the circular zero, were Indian inventions that traveled westward along the trade routes.

A MAJOR MATHEMATICIAN

Although Severus Sebokht wrote about the Indian numbers in the seventh century A.D., it took another two hundred years for this system to be accepted by the Islamic world. When the numerals from India became popular in the Moslem world during the ninth century, they were being enthusiastically praised by one of the greatest Moslem mathematicians. This was a person named Al-Khwarizmi (780–850), who was a giant of Islamic mathematics. His Latin name, Algorithmi, is today associated with any system of arithmetic based on the use of decimals.

Al-Khwarizmi was born in an area called Khwarizm that lay east of the Caspian Sea. He used his place of birth in his name as was the custom at that time in the Islamic world. In Baghdad, an important center of Islamic learning, Al-Khwarizmi wrote glowing accounts of the numbers from India and encouraged their use in all calculations. His books include one titled *Al-Khwarizmi on the Numerals of the Indians* that did much to extend the use of these symbols throughout the Western world.

Al-Khwarizmi developed algebra as it is known today, refining the process from older forms used by the Greeks and Egyptians. He also introduced the name into the language, writing about *al-jabr*. This is an Arabic word that means "restitution." In algebra a mathematician substitutes symbols, such as x, y, or z, for numbers in order to solve certain types of problems.

Algebra is a process used when some information is known about a problem and other things are not. The letters are used for the unknown parts, which are set up in relationship to the things that are known. Such relationships, called equations, are then solved to supply the unknown information.

TRIGONOMETRY

Moslem mathematicians also improved upon older methods used when working with angles and triangles. The branch of mathematics dealing with angles and triangles, called **trigonometry**, is extremely important to surveyors and astronomers in their measurements of the space between objects on earth or in the skies.

Al-Khwarizmi did some of this work, but the major contributions came from another scholar, Al-Battani (850–929). Born the same year that Al-Khwarizmi died, Al-Battani became famous as one of the leading astronomers and mathematicians of Islam. He constructed tables giving the ratios between the sides of any right triangle (one containing an angle of 90 degrees). When two angles and the side between them are known, the remaining angle and the unknown sides of a right triangle can be found. This is also true if two sides and the angle between them are known.

Surveyors use trigonometry to figure out how far it is across a river or a swamp where an actual measurement is impossible. They do this by sighting an object (such as a tree or rock) on the other side. Then they turn at a right angle and measure a distance along their side of the river or swamp. Finally, they take a second sighting of the object and measure the second angle. This gives

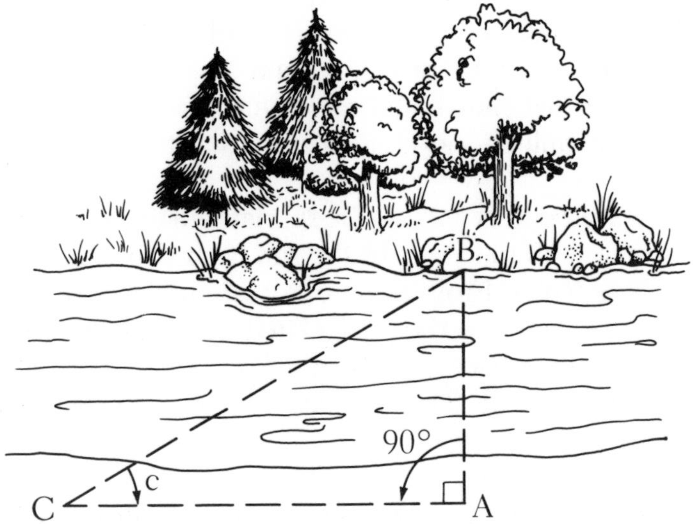

Fig. 1 Moslem surveyors could find the distance across a river using trigonometry. They set up a half-imaginary triangle with one right angle (90 degrees). They then measured the distance from A to C and the angle c. With this information they could then compute the distance across the river, between A and B.

them the two angles of the triangle they have created plus the length of the one side they have measured. Using trigonometry tables first calculated by Al-Battani and other Islamic mathematicians, modern surveyors can compute the unknown side of the triangle. This tells them how far it is across the river or swamp to the object they sighted on the other side.

MISSION: MEASURE THE EARTH

The size and shape of the earth had fascinated scientists since ancient times. Although most ordinary people thought the earth was flat, careful observers noticed things that led them to believe the earth was round. For example, some looked at the earth's shadow on the moon during an eclipse and saw that it was curved. Others noticed that they could see a ship's sails as it approached port before the hull appeared, indicating that the ship was sailing on a curved sea.

In the third century B.C. a Greek mathematician named Eratosthenes measured the angle of the sun from two different places along the Nile River. From these observations he concluded that the earth was round. He then calculated the distance around the earth (the circumference) at about 24,600 miles (39,400 km)—extremely close to the 24,900 miles (39,800 km) that scientists accept today.

Over a century later, around 100 B.C., another Greek astronomer, named Posidonius of Apamea, repeated Eratosthenes' work. Even though he used the same method, Posidonius reached a different conclusion. He thought the earth was only about 18,000 miles (29,000 km) in circumference.

This smaller figure was used by a Greek astronomer and geographer named Ptolemy, who lived in Alexandria in the second century A.D. Ptolemy went on to develop many maps using the 18,000-mile figure, so it became much better known than the more accurate figure calculated by Eratosthenes.

Accounts of these attempts to measure the earth were collected by Islamic scholars, who sought out all of the old scientific manuscripts they could find. These were taken to Baghdad, where in 830 a Moslem ruler named Al-Ma'mun built a huge center of learning called the House of Wisdom. Soon after he founded this center, Al-Ma'mun assigned the scholars there a major mission: they were to measure the size of the earth.

Following the procedures of Posidonius and Eratosthenes, the mathematicians at Baghdad measured the distance between two cities and found the angle of the sun from each of them. The Moslem scientists used correct procedures, but their actual measurements were flawed. As a result, they arrived at a figure of 20,400 miles (32,600 km) for the distance around the globe. This seemed to confirm the figure used by Ptolemy, so this mistaken belief that the world was only about 20,000 miles (32,000 km) in circumference was passed on to future generations.

Moslem scientists continued to search through the ancient manuscripts coming into Baghdad from the many countries that the Moslems conquered. From these they learned more and more about older scientific views of the world in which they lived.

3

STUDYING THE STARS

Many of the ancient manuscripts that Arab traders brought from foreign lands dealt with astronomy, the study of the stars and planets. They included extensive tables that showed the apparent movements of the heavenly bodies across the night skies as observed by the ancient stargazers of Greece, Persia, and India.

Al-Khwarizmi is said to have first become interested in the numbers from India when he found them in astronomical tables worked out there many centuries before. These charts were accurate and important, but the astronomical writings of the Greeks had even more influence on Islamic science.

The ancient Greeks had studied the skies and learned to predict eclipses as early as the sixth century B.C. By the third century B.C. they even speculated that the earth revolved around the sun, but that idea was lost for many centuries.

PTOLEMY'S SYSTEM

Instead, people followed an erroneous belief popularized by Ptolemy, the Greek astronomer and mapmaker in Alexandria who had used Posidonius' incorrect figures about the size of the earth. Ptolemy developed his own theory about the movements of the moon and planets. It placed the earth at the center of the universe. The sun, moon, and planets traveled around the earth in perfect circles, according to his system. These circular orbits did not always agree with a planet's observed position. To take care of this, Ptolemy invented additional movements for some planets so that their actual positions would agree with those in his theory.

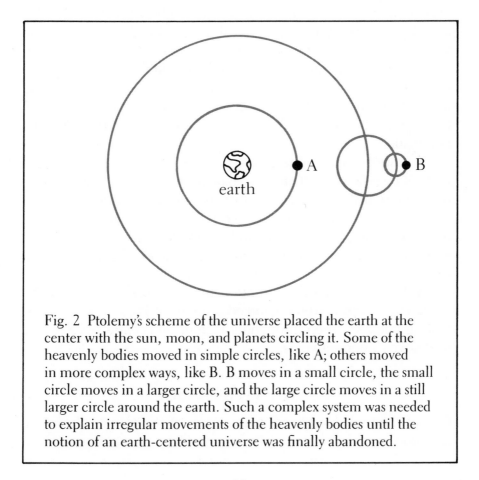

Fig. 2 Ptolemy's scheme of the universe placed the earth at the center with the sun, moon, and planets circling it. Some of the heavenly bodies moved in simple circles, like A; others moved in more complex ways, like B. B moves in a small circle, the small circle moves in a larger circle, and the large circle moves in a still larger circle around the earth. Such a complex system was needed to explain irregular movements of the heavenly bodies until the notion of an earth-centered universe was finally abandoned.

This created a complicated planetary system that few people understood even though most accepted it for the next fourteen hundred years. As long as one worked within the Ptolemaic system, all planetary movements seemed to be mathematically correct. This was true because the pattern that Ptolemy worked out was consistent within itself even though it was based on the mistaken idea that the earth was the center of the solar system.

Ptolemy drew up detailed tables to show each planet's movements. He gave the times when a planet rose and set on the earth's horizon as well as when it reached its highest point in the sky, called its **zenith**. The astronomical data of his theory of the universe was collected in a book that was later called the *Almagest*.

Moslem astronomers studied Ptolemy's tables and then began making their own observations. Since they were constantly trying to measure and catalog all things in nature, the astronomers of Islam gradually found and corrected many mistakes that Ptolemy had made.

An astronomical table giving the means to calculate the positions of the stars and planets is called a *zij* in Arabic. Each astronomer wrote his own *zij*, attempting to make it more accurate than those prepared earlier. He also wrote down comments about the universe, giving his theories and the new facts he discovered. Al-Khwarizmi was one of the scholars who worked out a detailed *zij*.

Al-Farghani, another ninth-century Moslem astronomer, wrote such a clear, well-organized account of Ptolemy's *Almagest* that his book was used throughout Europe and central Asia for the next seven hundred years.

THE ASTROLABE

One of the tools used to measure angles of the planets above the horizon was an instrument called an **astrolabe**. In its simplest form,

This zij, or table, gives information
on the constellations in the Zodiac.

it was a ring or a disk with the degrees of a circle marked on it and pointing arms that could be aimed at two different places to measure the angle between them. When turned on its side, the astrolabe was used to find the angle of a star or planet above the horizon. Moslem navigators and other sailors determined their latitude at sea by measuring the angle of the North Star above the horizon.

Al-Battani, the mathematician who developed trigonometry tables, used an early form of the astrolabe to make careful observations of planetary movements over a period of forty-one years. From these observations he was able to measure some of the regular intervals, called astronomical constants, that occur in the movements of heavenly bodies.

PLOTTING
THE SUN'S PATH

Since the days of the early Greeks, stargazers had observed the sun's apparent path across the sky and noted where it seems to cross the earth's equator. (It is called an apparent path because the sun only appears to move across the sky. In reality, it is the earth that moves.)

These apparent crossings of the equator by the sun occur twice a year, in March and September, at times called, respectively, the spring and fall **equinoxes**. Around these times, day and night are of equal length (the prefix *equi-* means "equal").

By the second century B.C., Greek astronomers had noted that the points where the sun's path, called the ecliptic, crosses the earth's equator seem to drift westward from year to year. This phenomenon, known as the precession of the equinoxes, is caused by the gravitational effect of the moon and sun on the earth. These influences cause the globe to wobble slightly like a top that one spins on the floor.

A *twelfth-century astrolabe*

Arabian astronomers and some of their tools

Both the precession of the equinoxes and the angle of the ecliptic are called astronomical constants because they change only negligibly with time. It would be several centuries before scientists explained the reasons for these occurrences, but Al-Battani was able to measure them correctly. He found the westward drift of the equinox to be 54.5 seconds of a degree each year. (There are 60 seconds in each minute and 60 minutes in each degree.) He also correctly measured the angle of the ecliptic to the earth's equator, finding it to be approximately 23 degrees, 5 minutes. Both of these measurements are close to the values accepted today.

Al-Battani put these and other astronomical constants into a *zij* and wrote about how he arrived at his figures so that others could use these methods in their work. In doing this, Al-Battani was helping to establish a procedure that has become an important part of modern science. This method of faithfully reporting one's observations and experiments allows others to check them for accuracy.

CREATING A CALENDAR

An important use of any data collected when observing the stars and planets is the creation of a more accurate calendar for use on earth. Farmers use calendars to tell them when it is safe to plant crops without the risk of a freeze, and travelers crossing mountains to trade in foreign lands need to know when the danger of snows in the high passes is over.

One of the most accurate calendars ever devised was created by an Islamic astronomer named Omar ibn al-Khayyami (1048–1131), better known today as Omar Khayyam and as the author of a famous Persian poem called the *Rubayyat*. Al-Khayyami was born in Persia and lived in several central Asian cities until he was invited at the age of twenty-two to take charge of an observatory in the city of Isfahan in Persia.

The constellations Ophiuchus (the man) and
Serpens (the serpent), depicted in a
tenth-century manuscript written by Al-Sufi

While there, he used his careful observations of the sun, moon, and planets to devise a calendar that had an error of only one day in five thousand years. This calendar, which was never widely used because people did not want to give up older, more familiar (but less reliable) ones, was more accurate than our calendar is today.

From observatories such as the one where Al-Khayyami worked in central Asia to others in distant Egypt, North Africa, and Spain, Islamic astronomers continued to study the movements of the stars and planets for several centuries. During that time some of them came close to discovering the fallacy of Ptolemy's system that placed the earth at the center of the universe. The data they recorded would help future astronomers arrive at a much more accurate view of the universe than the model the ancient Greeks had passed along to the Moslem scientists.

LOOKING INTO VISION

Moslem astronomers were generally content to follow Ptolemy's view of the universe, but in other fields the scientists of Islam broke with older, incorrect theories. Their original research was outstanding in the branch of physics called **optics**, the study of light and vision.

The scholar who contributed most in this field was Ibn al-Haytham (c. 965–1039). (Accurate records of births and deaths were seldom kept, so many such dates are only approximate. This is indicated by using either a question mark or the letter c, which stands for the Latin word *circa*, meaning "about" or "around.")

Known to later generations by the Latin name Alhazen (after his first name, al-Hasan), Ibn al-Haytham was an all-around intellectual giant who made major contributions in the fields of mathematics, astronomy, medicine, and engineering. He was already famous for his work in several fields before he began studying optics when he was past fifty.

ENGINEERING NEEDS

Ibn al-Haytham was born in Basra, a city east of the Tigris and Euphrates rivers. Irrigation is a matter of life or death in that part of the Middle East, where much of the area is dry and nonproductive until water is brought to the fields. Huge canal systems, too big for individuals to manage, were maintained for centuries by the governments involved.

One of Islam's largest irrigation and flood-control projects was in the Tigris-Euphrates river valleys near where Ibn al-Haytham grew up. The Euphrates River had been channeled many years before into Mesopotamia on the west, and the Tigris had been diverted into Persia on the east. A great canal connected the two rivers at Baghdad, and lesser canals carried irrigation water to the smaller communities and on to the individual farms and orchards throughout the area.

Ibn al-Haytham was familiar with these irrigation systems and the details of their maintenance when he was ordered to go to Cairo in Egypt early in the eleventh century. A competing line of caliphs (the Moslem term for leaders of the faith) had established their capital of the Moslem world in Egypt, where they built the city of Cairo on the banks of the Nile River.

There in 1005 a caliph named Al-Hakim also constructed a huge center of learning, which he called the House of Knowledge. It had an observatory and a library that some accounts say contained over a million handwritten books. Al-Hakim wanted Ibn al-Haytham to come to the House of Knowledge, and the scholar complied. In Egypt, Ibn al-Haytham took an immediate interest in the annual floods along the Nile River, telling the caliph that these overflows could be prevented. He led an expedition up the Nile to find a place where such flood-control measures could be installed.

As he traveled upstream, Ibn al-Haytham saw the marvelous temples and other buildings that the ancient Egyptians had constructed. By the time he reached the area where the modern Aswan High Dam is located, it was obvious to him what great engineers the ancient people of Egypt had been. He realized that if there was a way to control the river's periodic floods, the Egyptians would have found it long ago. With this realization came the knowledge that his idea was wrong and his great project would have to be abandoned.

Knowing that Al-Hakim beheaded people who failed to deliver the results they had promised, Ibn al-Haytham went into hiding until the caliph died. Then he reappeared in Cairo, where he began studying light and optics during his mid-fifties. This led to experiments that would make his name famous.

THE SECRET OF SIGHT

In the fourth century B.C. Greek philosophers had said that people see because their eyes send out a ray of vision that makes this possible. Ptolemy went along with this view, which meant that it was accepted by nearly everyone. A Greek physician named Galen, who lived late in the second century A.D., had other ideas, but his views in this matter were generally ignored.

Galen believed that sight had something to do with the lens of the eye. He even theorized that a nerve connects the eye with the brain to make vision possible. Ibn al-Haytham accepted Galen's concept as his starting point. Rejecting the ideas of the ancient Greeks and Ptolemy, Ibn al-Haytham began a series of experiments to test the way light travels through translucent substances (things that light passes through, such as glass, water, and ice.)

Ibn al-Haytham developed the idea that light is emitted by all radiant sources; that it travels in straight lines; and that it falls on

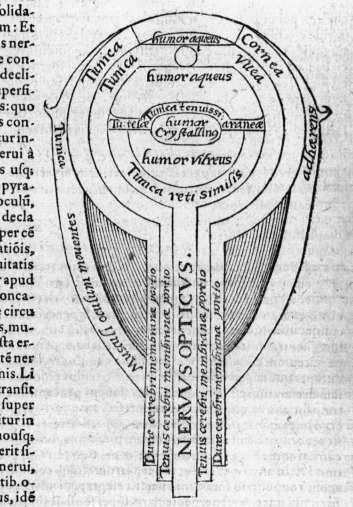

A Western edition of Al-Haytham's study of the eye.
You can probably make out the Latin words humor (humor),
cornea (cornea), and nervus opticus (optic nerve).

objects and is reflected back to the eye, making sight possible. This was the beginning of the modern view about light and vision.

From his studies of light traveling through different translucent and transparent substances, Ibn al-Haytham explained the phenomenon known as refraction of light. This is what makes a stick appear to bend when one end is in the water. Ibn al-Haytham correctly explained that this happens because light travels at different speeds through air and water, moving slightly slower in water. The portion of the stick below the surface of the water is thrown slightly out of line with the part that remains above the waterline.

Since the time of ancient Greece, humankind had known about something called a camera obscura effect. This is the technique of darkening a room and then making a tiny hole through which light can enter. An inverted image of the scene outside will appear on the wall opposite the small opening. It is, of course, the principle that makes possible modern photography.

Ibn al-Haytham experimented with the camera obscura phenomenon in order to arrive at his idea that light always travels in a straight line. He came close to actually inventing the lens and with it the basic idea of the telescope and microscope. However, this remained for others to accomplish in the sixteenth century.

THE RAINBOW EFFECT

One aspect of optics that had fascinated humankind since early times was the rainbow. How could sunlight produce this beautiful effect? And why did the colors always appear in the same order, with red on top and violet at the bottom? Ibn al-Haytham wrestled unsuccessfully with these questions; they would be answered by one of his followers, a Persian named Al-Farisi (died 1320), who wrote commentaries on Ibn al-Haytham's work and studied his experiments in detail.

Al-Farisi noted the similarity between the raindrop and a glass sphere, and that gave him the idea he needed. Working in a darkened room, Al-Farisi made a series of investigations with a round glass filled with water. Observing what happened when sunlight was allowed to shine in through a small opening and then pass through the round container of water (which he compared with a raindrop), he explained how rainbows are produced.

Al-Farisi wrote that raindrops act like tiny mirrors, both reflecting and refracting the light from the sun. In the process, light is separated into colors. He pointed out that sunshine enters the drop of water and is bent (refracted). Then it is reflected within the raindrop before it finally shines on a wall (or on a cloud out-of-doors). Al-Farisi's round container worked like a raindrop, producing the same red-through-violet colors that appear in natural rainbows.

The work of Ibn al-Haytham and Al-Farisi laid the groundwork for those who would come after them, providing accurate explanations of the phenomena they studied. Even more important, both of them obtained their results through the use of experimental methods instead of blindly following the theories and methods of Plato, Aristotle, Ptolemy, and others who had gone before them.

This use of experimental methods, together with the practice of making careful measurements of natural things, was the beginning of a major transformation in the way scientists studied the world of nature. In writing about his experiments with light in a volume called the *Book of Optics*, Ibn al-Haytham explained this new approach to science. He left behind a legacy of experiments with light and optics that provided a starting point for the scholars of the Western **Renaissance**. (*Renaissance* means "rebirth.") The term is used to describe the period in the fourteenth to sixteenth centuries when a renewal of interest in science and art began in the West.

Ibn al-Haytham's legacy of step-by-step experimental methods has led modern experts to consider this man who failed to control the floods along the Nile River to be the greatest physicist that Islam ever produced and one of the greatest students of optics the world has ever known.

5

MYSTERY OF THE MIDNIGHT SUN

At the same time that Ibn al-Haytham was studying light and vision, another great scholar was collecting information about the many distant lands touched by Moslem traders. His name was Al-Biruni (973–1048?), and he was destined to be called one of Islam's wisest scholars.

In the tenth century Al-Biruni had many travelers' accounts to choose from. Arab caravans connected Baghdad with such distant Asian lands as India and China. Moslem ships dominated the Mediterranean Sea, sailing west from Cairo to Spain and Morocco. Some overland trade routes stretched north to Great Britain and Scandinavia; others reached as far south as Ethiopia. Arabic coins have been found among the Eskimos of Lapland as well as in Chinese cities of the Far East. Traders and travelers introduced Persian words such as *caravan* and *bazaar* into the European languages, along with such Arabic ones as *magazine* and *check*.

Many accounts of these travels were written, plus descriptions of the exotic lands that merchants visited. One of the best known of these is a ninth-century narrative about a seafarer that has come down to us as *Sinbad the Sailor*.

THE ERRATIC SULTAN

Some of the stories told by travelers were less welcome because they clashed with Moslem beliefs. In 1024 Sultan Mahmud, who ruled a huge area in central Asia called Ghazna, was at first fascinated by the accounts of some visitors who arrived from Arctic areas. These foreigners, who sought a trading alliance with the sultan, spoke of great white bears whose coats blended into the snowy mountain slopes where they roamed. They also described people who dressed in furs and fished through the ice for their food.

Next, these visitors, who were describing the Eskimos of the far north, mentioned something unbelievable. They told of long summer days when the sun continued to shine for months at a time.

Angrily the sultan ordered them to retract this statement. Such a thing could not be! When the Prophet Mohammed had told the faithful to pray five times each day, he had specified prayers between daybreak and sunrise and again between sunset and dark. How could people fulfill these instructions in a land where the sun neither rose nor set?

At this point Al-Biruni, who was one of the sultan's advisers, came to the visitors' rescue. He had collected many other accounts about the land of the midnight sun, and he convinced the erratic ruler that his visitors were telling the truth. Al-Biruni explained that the earth's axis is tilted, and the sun strikes at a different angle farther north than it does in the lands of the south. This causes long summer days in the far north, and in winter it results in long nights with no sunshine at all.

The sultan would not have listened to a lesser person, but he respected Al-Biruni's knowledge. This trusted adviser knew about many things that no one else could hope to comprehend. By the time of this incident in 1024, Al-Biruni had already written millions of words on subjects ranging from astronomy and arithmetic through history and mapmaking to religion, magic, and medicine.

A PERSON OF
MANY TALENTS

Who was this person who had such a wide range of knowledge? Al-Biruni was born in 973 in a small town northeast of Khiva, the birthplace of Al-Khwarizmi. Nothing is known about his childhood, but by the time he was a teenager Al-Biruni had begun to study under a well-known astronomer and mathematician named Abu Nasr Mansur. At seventeen he built a ring that was divided into halves of degrees, and he used it to determine the latitude of the town of Kath east of the Caspian Sea in central Asia.

Four years later Al-Biruni built a much larger ring and planned to observe the sun on the longest day of the year—the summer solstice—at a place near Kath. He hoped to begin a series of observations that would lead to better measurements of the earth's actual size. Civil war broke out, and he was forced to flee. Two years later he observed and measured an eclipse of the moon near the city of Rayy in the same area of central Asia, and another astronomer made similar observations at Baghdad. Comparing the exact time of the eclipse at those two places, they calculated their difference in longitude, just as navigators now compute their position at sea by comparing local sun time with that of the Greenwich Observatory in England.

A POWERFUL PATRON

Al-Biruni tried to make additional astronomical observations in the area east of the Caspian Sea where the present countries of Iran, Afghanistan, and the U.S.S.R. touch one another. He hoped that

41

these observations would allow him to make more accurate maps, but political unrest in the region kept interfering with his work. Into this turmoil stepped Sultan Mahmud, who ruled Ghazna, a city in the area now occupied by Afghanistan. He had conquered the entire area from Mesopotamia to India, setting up an empire that stretched 1,000 miles (1,600 km) from north to south and twice that distance from east to west.

The sultan sought out the wisest people of the time and gathered them around him, as Al-Ma'mun had done in ninth-century Baghdad. Al-Biruni was one of the first to be chosen, and he followed Mahmud of Ghazna on a conquest of India that extended Moslem rule farther southeast than it had ever gone before. Everywhere he went, Al-Biruni observed, recorded, and wrote about the natural features of the land, the people and their customs, and any new plants or animals he discovered. He also measured the latitude and longitude of cities, rivers, and mountains that he mapped along the way.

At a mountain near the city of Nandana on the major route into the Indus Valley, Al-Biruni made a series of astronomical observations like those performed much earlier at the House of Wisdom in Baghdad. With the use of trigonometry he hoped to make his own estimate of the size of the earth, but details of the project, including his results, have been lost.

Al-Biruni's calculations of the latitude and longitude of various places he visited was a continuation of the tradition of Islamic science that sought to observe and measure all kinds of phenomena in the natural world. His work, along with that of other Islamic scientists, also allowed the Moslems to create more accurate maps than the world had known before their time.

MAPS AND MAPMAKERS

Accurate maps were important to the Moslem traders who traveled throughout the world. In the ninth century Al-Khwarizmi made one of the Islamic world's first atlases. He called this volume the *Book on the Form of the Earth*. In it he listed the longitudes of different places and gave lengths of daylight at many locations.

Longitude was listed in degrees and minutes east or west of a designated prime meridian, as it is on modern maps. (Today's mapmakers use the prime meridian at Greenwich Observatory near London, England.) Instead of using lines of latitude as geographers do today, Moslem mapmakers listed the length of daylight at cities on the summer solstice, which occurs around June 21 or 22. If the length of daylight on this day was the same at a city in Spain and at a town in central Asia, the mapmakers of Islam correctly assumed that the two places were the same distance north of the equator.

Al-Khwarizmi included a map in his atlas that appears to have been taken from a book of Ptolemy's called *Geographia*. Ptolemy, who had formulated the theory of the earth-centered solar system, also laid down principles for mapmaking on earth. These included instructions on how to divide a large world map into regional sections. They also told how to use longitude lines on a map. Most Islamic atlases followed his system. On the opening page there was a map of the known world, showing it as a disk surrounded by water. Separate maps of individual regions represented various Islamic countries and marked the major trade routes across them.

By the twelfth century a mapmaker named Al-Idrisi (c. 1100–1166) began preparing atlases in a huge Moslem cultural center that had been created at Cordova in Spain. A native of Ceuta in Morocco, Al-Idrisi set off at the age of sixteen to travel through Asia Minor. He also visited parts of Europe, including Spain and southern France, and traveled north to England in search of information about that country.

In addition to his own travels, Al-Idrisi collected older atlases that traders brought to him and used them as sources of information for new maps that he made. Such information provided gen-

Al-Idrisi's map of the world

eral impressions about the many lands that Moslem traders visited, but mapmakers needed exact details of the latitude and longitude of different cities. They could get such details only from exact observations of the type that Al-Biruni made whenever he traveled anywhere in the world.

After his long trip to India, Al-Biruni continued to travel, taking time to note the exact details about places he visited, until he was past seventy. Some historians say he was alive and working for several years after the date of 1048 that is usually given for his death. These accounts report that he lived until he was well past eighty and worked right up to the time of his death.

During his long life he wrote 146 different works in all. Many of these have been lost, but their size and subject matter are known from indexes made at the time. Scholars estimate that Al-Biruni's total written output would fill over thirteen thousand pages set in small type, or the equivalent of more than half of an encyclopedia the size of the Britannica or the Americana.

His major surviving work is a seven-hundred-page book on India. It describes the people and their legends, history, religion, philosophy, and life-styles as well as the geology and geography of this varied subcontinent. Other books deal with mathematics, philosophy, medicine, and religion.

These works show the great scope of Al-Biruni's life and work, which is so broad that modern scholars consider this man who once explained the midnight sun to the sultan to be one of the wisest people that Islam ever produced.

6

SEARCH FOR THE SECRETS OF LIFE

Another Moslem scientist, who lived about the same time as Al-Biruni, became one of Islam's leading physicians. This was Ibn Sina (980–1037). Like Al-Biruni, he distinguished himself while still a teenager.

Al-Biruni built his first astrolabe and began making astronomical observations at the age of seventeen. At the same age, Ibn Sina cured a local ruler's stomachache. Just as Al-Biruni's teenage interest in astronomy and geography led to a lifetime interest in those scientific fields, Ibn Sina's early medical endeavors grew into a lifelong career in medicine.

Ibn Sina, who would be known throughout medieval Europe by the Latinized form of his name, Avicenna, was born in central Asia in 980, just seven years after the birth of Al-Biruni. By the age of ten Ibn Sina had memorized the entire Koran, Islam's sacred book of Mohammed's teachings, and had studied everything he could find on medicine and other branches of science and philosophy.

When he was seventeen, Ibn Sina went to see a sultan named Ibn Mansur, who ruled his native city of Bukhara. The sultan had

Ibn Sina and his students

hundreds of people at his command, but none could do anything about the digestive problems that made his life miserable. In desperation he accepted the help of this seventeen-year-old who claimed he could cure his stomachache.

Miraculously, Ibn Mansur got better, and in gratitude he offered Ibn Sina any reward he wanted. To his surprise, the only thing the youth cared about was the sultan's huge library. With the ruler's permission he began reading through volume after volume, avidly absorbing the knowledge these books contained.

SECRETS OF HEALING

The search for knowledge would always be Ibn Sina's main interest. The son of an official in Bukhara, he came from a family that loved and valued learning. Like Al-Biruni, Ibn Sina was called to serve Mahmud of Ghazna as one of his wise men. Unlike the other man, Ibn Sina refused to have anything to do with the tyrant and fled into the desert. Later he accepted political appointments from other rulers, but he often made enemies and was sometimes put into jail because of his freethinking and sharp tongue.

Between government appointments, jail, and various commitments, Ibn Sina operated a series of free clinics to help sick and injured people. He believed that many human health problems are caused by things people do that interfere with the body's natural healing processes—as when we keep on using a sore arm instead of resting it or when we fail to get enough sleep when fighting off a cold. Many of the treatments Ibn Sina designed involved the use of herbs, hot baths, and even major surgery to remove some internal blockage within the patient's body, restoring the person's system to its natural balance.

In the past, doctors who had such theories were content to reason about them and argue with one another over such ideas. Ibn Sina went further and tested his medical ideas in the free clinics he had established.

Wherever he was—in hiding, in jail, or at a clinic—Ibn Sina wrote constantly about medicine, philosophy, and other things he observed. His total output includes some 270 different works of various lengths, some actually dictated while he rode on horseback into battle with a ruler he was serving at the time.

One of his best known works is a multivolume book called *The Canon of Medicine*. Over a million words long, it summarizes the history and traditions of medical practice for more than a thousand years before his time. Another major work is a multivolume encyclopedia covering the entire field of human knowledge.

While working on his writings, Ibn Sina suffered severe pains in his abdomen. During the forty years since he had treated the sultan in Bukhara, Ibn Sina had cured many other people's stomachaches, but his own pains failed to respond to any of his treatments. The great doctor died in 1037, three years before his sixtieth birthday.

ANOTHER GREAT DOCTOR

Two portraits of Moslem physicians hung for centuries in the University of Paris School of Medicine. One was, of course, that of Ibn Sina. The other was of Al-Razi, a doctor who lived nearly a century earlier.

Known in Latin as Rhazes, Al-Razi was born in Persia about 865, and he died sometime around 925 or 926. He excelled in powers of observation and wrote some 184 different works on what he learned as a practicing doctor. Al-Razi's most important work is a 20-volume book that covers every branch of medicine. A smaller book, called simply *Treatise on Smallpox and Measles*, is also a masterpiece of direct observation of these illnesses. It is the first accurate study of infectious disease available in the West.

Al-Razi and Ibn Sina were part of a long tradition of medical practice that went back to the early days of Moslem rule. In the year 707, just seventy-six years after the Prophet's death, the Moslems founded a hospital in Damascus. They staffed it with doctors paid by the government, and it provided a full range of hospital services. This became the model for other such institutions established throughout the Islamic world.

INSTRUCTION AND EXAMINATIONS

Medical instruction was given in these hospitals, and doctors were required to pass examinations monitored by the state. Druggists and barbers (who often bled people as a medical treatment) were also subject to regulation in many cities.

Hospitals in Moslem countries treated both men and women, in separate wards, and were either totally financed or generously supported by the government. In the tenth century this hospital system was extended to serve rural areas, people in prisons, and residents of inner-city areas, a practice unheard of at that time outside Moslem countries.

Medical practice in these hospitals was based on information that had been gathered from the Greeks, the Persians, and the people of India. These ancient books included folklore about herbs and drugs that were said to relieve certain ailments. To this the Islamic doctors added their own experience.

A physician named Al-Dinawari (815–895) collected all of the information he could find on medical plants known in pre-Islamic Arabia. He added the uses developed by Moslem doctors and combined this information in a volume called the *Book of Plants*. Both Al-Biruni and Ibn Sina also wrote extensively about the medicinal use of plants in their day. Ibn Sina listed some 760 herbs and drugs in *The Canon of Medicine*.

The preparations available to Moslem doctors included sedatives, which help people to relax. They also used hashish, a much stronger narcotic made from hemp plants, as a painkiller after surgery. By the tenth century a Moslem doctor in Spain named Al-Zahrawi (936–c. 1013) began using antiseptics to cleanse wounds, a practice unheard of in the Western world until the nineteenth century. Al-Zahrawi also devised sutures made from animal intestines and silk to sew up surgical cuts, and he designed many surgical instruments, including knives, scalpels, probes, hooks, and other devices used during operations.

A MAJOR MEDICAL BREAKTHROUGH

One of the greatest breakthroughs in medical knowledge was made by Moslem doctors who lived about two hundred years after Ibn Sina's death. This was the discovery that blood circulates throughout the body, a line of thought contrary to ancient medical beliefs.

The doctor who made the breakthrough was a native of Syria named Ibn an-Nafis (c. 1210–1288). Ibn an-Nafis boldly contradicted the theories of Galen, the second-century Greek physician. Galen had written that blood was manufactured in the liver as needed by the body and that it flowed back and forth between the left and right sides of the heart. Ibn an-Nafis said Galen was wrong about this.

Ibn an-Nafis wrote that the right side of the heart pumps blood to the lungs, where it is purified. The blood then returns to the left side of the heart, which pumps it out through the arteries to the rest of the body. It passes through the veins and returns to the right side of the heart, where the process starts over again.

He had no idea how the blood got from the arteries to the veins. That remained for his contemporary, Ibn al-Quff (1233–1286), to explain. Ibn al-Quff taught medicine and practiced in hospitals in and around Damascus and other cities of the Holy Land. Much of his work involved surgery on the wounds of dying

r couerſatus eſt in diſpoñibus ſuis. τ nõ fecit ei þricatē in
ambulatione nocumentū oīno. ¶ Si aūt os eminēs in lo-
co corporis iam fractũ eſt:tũc oportet vt ſerres ipſm ſm hunc
modũ:τ ẽ vt accipias ligamēturē ſtringe ipſm in extremita-
te oſſis eminētis:τ pụtpe alicui ẹ extẽdat ipſm ad ſurſum:τ
pone ligamẽtũ aliud ex lana groſſi ligameto p̃. Deinde li-
ga ipſm ſup carne ẽ ẽ ſub oſſe:τ extẽde extremitatē eius:vt
trahas carnē ad inferiora:τ tu detegis carnē ſup locũ quẽ
vis ſerrare:vt nõ ledat ſerra carnē:pone lignũ aut tabulaṁ
ſub oſſe iſt io:decēter:qñ qn facis illo:nõ phibet qn ſecet
carnẽ corruptā. Et oportet vt ſit ſerratura ſup locũ corruptum
parū:ut vt nõ ſit i þcauitate oſſis corruptio:τ nõ appareat
in apparitiõe ſue ſenſui:τ cogat ad ſerraturã ſui vice alia.
¶ Quõ ſi os eſt corruptũ τ nõ eſt eminēs:tũc þtinuat pars
ei:τ cũ pte:τ corruptio ẽ in medio ei? aut in pte ipſi:tũc de-
rege car nẽ ab oſtine pṙib? totã. Deinde pone lignũ inferi?.
poſtea ſerra illud ex pte þ vbi ẽ corruptio:donec þtinuet
ſerratura ex pte altera:τ ſit ſerratura ſm lõgitudinẽ a cor-
ruptioe pariup erſcõm qp dixim?. ¶ Quõ ſi corruptio eſt in
ſuctura incide ipſam iuncturã corruptã τ ſerra os vbi cõti-
nuat ex pte altera. Si ro corruptio eſt in þtinuatioe quap
iunctura:tũc nõ eſt in ea igenũ niſi abraſio. ¶ Quõ ſi corruptio eſt in pectine manus:aut in pectine pedis:tũc res in
eo eſt difficilis valde. Uerū oportet vt inquiras corruptioē ali-
ter apparearat tibi. Et abradas eam:τ mūdes ipſa3 ſm quã-
cũ3 diſpoſitiõe tibi poſſe eſt:τ cũ quocũ3 ingenio. recti-
ficat tibi:τ n facit tibi þrietatē venà:aut neruus. ¶ Et
ſcias ẹ inciſioia:τ ſerre ad incidendũ iſta oſſa ſunt multa:
ſm ſitũ oſſium:τ preparationē eoꝛ τ ipſoꝛ groſſitudinẽ:τ
ſubtilitatem eoꝛ:τ magnitudinē:τ paruitatē ipſoꝛ:τ ſm
ricem ipſoꝛ:τ eoꝛum raritatem. Quapropter oportet vt þ-
pares omni ſpeciei operatiõis inſtrumentũ þueniẽs ad illã
operationē. ¶ Et ſcias ẹ operatiões iſte ſignificat tibi ſuper ſpeciē inſtrumēti quo indiges quãdo tecũ eſt ſtudium
longum. Et cognitio modoꝛ huius artis teſtimoniũ modoꝛ egritudinũ:tũc enim iam inueniens per teipſum illud
quod þuenit ei ex inſtrumētis ad oẽm infirmitatē. Et ego
ſum firmans tibi in vltimo huius capituli numeꝛ inſtroꝛ
que pones exempla ſuper que incides. τ þbationem qua
experiaris ſuper alia. **Forma ſerre.**

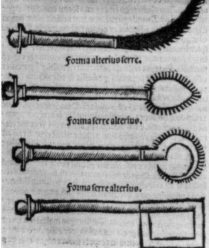

Forma alterius ſerre.

Forma ſerre alterius.

Forma ſerre alterius.

Sit caput huius raſoꝛij:ſm formam capitis claui ſtellatis
τ puncta eius ſit ſm formam punctoꝛ eliſcherbegi. Et non
þuenit niſi vt fricentur cum eo capita iuncturãꝝ:qñ coꝛ-
rumpuntur aut os amplum magnum.
Forma maioris raſoꝛij.

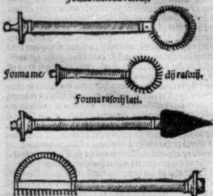

Forma me- dij raſoꝛij.

Forma raſoꝛij lati.

Hec forma ſerre depicta ſit decēter facta.fiat arcus eius ſu-
perioꝛ acutias eius ex ferro:τ manubriũ eius ex buſſo:
τ piramidale decenter factum.
Forma raſoꝛij in quo eſt concauitas.

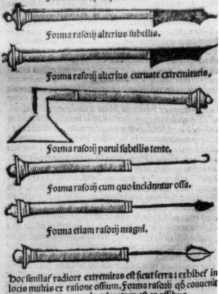

Forma raſoꝛij alterius ſubtilis.

Forma raſoꝛij alterius curuate extremitatis.

Forma raſoꝛij parui ſubtilis tente.

Forma raſoꝛij cum quo incidantur oſſa.

Forma etiam raſoꝛij magni.

Hoc ſimilas radioꝛ extremitas eſt ſicut ſerra: exhibet in
locis multis ex raſione oſſium. Forma raſoꝛij qð þuenit
ad raſionem eius quod perforatum eſt ex oſſibus.

Islamic soldiers who fought against Christian Crusaders trying to capture Jerusalem and other holy places.

During this period Ibn al-Quff wrote that tiny capillaries allowed the blood to flow from the arteries to the veins. He also described the function of the **cardial valves** in the veins and heart chambers. These are valves that open in only one direction, keeping the blood flowing the same way throughout the entire circulatory system.

Islamic medicine had many other firsts, including the use of **tourniquets** to stop arterial bleeding as early as the tenth century. Many of these discoveries were lost and then rediscovered much later by Western medicine. However, the scope of Islamic medical knowledge and the careful investigations that went into the healing arts in Moslem hospitals advanced medicine far beyond anything seen in the Western world until that time.

MYSTERIES OF ALCHEMY

While many Islamic doctors looked for a relationship between humankind and nature only within their patients' bodies, Al-Razi and a few others followed another path in their search for a way to ensure health and happiness. This was an alternate route called **alchemy,** an experimental process that gradually changed into modern chemistry.

Alchemists believed that they could discover solutions for most of humanity's problems. Working secretly in crude, dark laborato-

Some of Al-Zahrawi's surgical instruments, drawn and described in a sixteenth-century Latin manuscript

ries, they performed experiments based on formulas and philosophies that had been handed down from generation to generation since the days of ancient China.

Some of the oldest writings about alchemy came from China; others originated in India. Centuries before the Islamic world was created by Mohammed's prophecies, the knowledge of alchemy had traveled overland from China and India to Persia and Egypt. Egyptian alchemists searched for ways to prolong life as far back as the times of the pharaohs. Their ancient art then moved on to Greece, where practitioners experimented with ways to find what they called a magic **elixir of life**. This was a substance that would restore youth and prolong life indefinitely.

Alchemists also sought ways to change base metals, such as lead and zinc, into gold. Although some of the people who said they could do this were interested only in cheating kings or other rich people out of their money, many sincerely believed that such a change was possible. All around them they saw mysterious transformations taking place. Metalsmiths could combine copper with zinc carbonate to produce a new metal that looked like gold. This mixture, called brass today, seemed to prove that one metal could be converted into another.

Arsenic was especially versatile. A mixture of about 2 percent arsenic and 98 percent copper produced a beautiful golden-colored metal. If the percentage of arsenic was increased to 4½ percent, the result was a shiny, silverlike substance. Since these changes were possible, it seemed that only time and patience were necessary to find a combination of materials that would create real gold out of cheaper base substances.

Al-Razi and other Islamic scientists read all of the ancient texts about alchemy that came into centers like the House of Wisdom. Then they performed experiments of their own to try to find magical substances that would prolong life or change base metals into gold. One of the leading Moslem alchemists wrote under the name

Jabir ibn Hayyan in the late eighth and early ninth centuries. So many texts on alchemy were written in this name that some scholars of today think Ibn Hayyan refers to the work of an entire school of philosophers instead of the output of only one man.

SCIENCE AND PHILOSOPHY

Alchemists and others searching for the meaning of life tended to belong to one or the other of two ancient systems of belief. One was that of the Greek philosopher Plato (427?–347 B.C.) and the other that of his chief pupil, Aristotle (384–322 B.C.).

Plato believed in unchanging, absolute values that give meaning to everyone's existence. He told people to look within themselves to find the important things of life, such as love and beauty. Today people speak of Platonic love or beauty when talking about the ideal forms of these qualities.

Aristotle concentrated on knowledge that can be found by searching outside ourselves and examining the world around us. He stressed experience and experimentation as the way to discover truths about nature. This is the way that modern science looks for answers.

For centuries Islamic scholars argued about whether one should follow Plato's suggestion and look within for truth or use experimental methods as Aristotle suggested. Some attempted to find ways of thinking that would combine both of these approaches into one philosophy. One of the first Moslem scholars to attempt this was Al-Kindi (c. 801–866). A participant in Baghdad's House of Wisdom, Al-Kindi wrote about astronomy, mathematics, and medicine as well as philosophy. Both Al-Razi and Ibn Sina followed his lead in attempting to combine the Platonic and Aristotelian ways of looking at the universe.

Aristotle's experimental approach was championed by an

Islamic physician named Ibn Rushd (1126–1198). Known by the Latin name Averroes, Ibn Rushd totally rejected Ibn Sina's views, along with the beliefs of Plato. Instead, he favored Aristotle's experimental approach. Ibn Rushd insisted that the truth about the universe can be found only through observation and experimentation.

Moslem science was pulled back and forth between the Platonic and Aristotelian approaches to learning. In actual practice, Aristotle's way of thinking dominated Islamic science, at least during its early period of greatness. This emphasis on experimental methods would be one of its great contributions to modern science as it exists today.

THE HERITAGE OF THE EARLY ISLAMIC SCIENTISTS

An eagerness to experiment and find new truths about the natural world marked the high point of Islamic science, which flowered for over 500 years, from the middle of the eighth century to the midpoint of the thirteenth. Then conflicting tides of philosophy within the faith, combined with challenges from outside the Islamic world, began to interfere with some of its scientists' most promising research work.

By the time Ibn Rushd died in 1198, strong currents were running against the freedom of thought so necessary for scientific development. Ignoring Mohammed's teachings about the importance of seeking knowledge throughout the world, religious fanatics began to restrict scientific work when the results contradicted their own ideas. Many important books were burned because the ideas they contained conflicted with those held by a local ruler.

EXTERNAL FORCES

Enemies of the Moslems had been pressing against their borders. Christian Crusaders captured Jerusalem in 1099, only to lose it again a century later. In Spain the Crusaders conquered Cordova, one of the wealthiest cities in all of Europe with its great mosque, cultural center, and library that contained half a million books.

An even greater outside threat came from the east, where war-like tribesmen began attacking the Moslem world in the twelfth and thirteenth centuries. Armies from Mongolia in north-central Asia captured Baghdad in 1258 and burned much of the city. It was rebuilt, only to be captured again in 1400 by another Mongolian conqueror.

Many of the scientific discoveries made by Moslem researchers were lost during this period of war and destruction. These included knowledge about the use of antiseptics and anesthesia in surgery and many other medical practices that Western scientists and doctors would independently rediscover in the nineteenth century.

ACCOMPLISHMENTS

Other discoveries made by Moslem doctors were preserved and used in Europe's developing medical schools. Ibn Sina's great *Canon of Medicine* was translated into Latin in the twelfth century, and it became the basic text used in the medical schools of Europe for the next 500 years. Al-Razi's 20-volume work on medicine and his smaller book on smallpox and measles were both translated into Latin and used for centuries in the same medical schools.

European scholars also made extensive use of other Islamic sources. The material gathered from travelers by the twelfth-century mapmaker Al-Idrisi, as well as his mapping technique, was used in Europe until replaced by newer approaches in the sixteenth century. The work of Ibn al-Haytham and Al-Farisi, representing as it did the first original thought in the field of optics since the time of ancient Greece, provided a sound foundation on which

A seventeenth-century microscope

Roger Bacon, Leonardo di Vinci, and others could build in the thirteenth, fourteenth, and fifteenth centuries. The work of the Islamic physicists with refraction of light laid the groundwork for European scholars to develop lenses for use in telescopes and microscopes. These instruments were invented in Europe around the beginning of the seventeenth century.

Islamic science also explored other areas where major breakthroughs would be made within a few centuries. Al-Damiri, an Egyptian philosopher and theologian who died in 1405, outlined the basic concepts of a theory about the survival of those animal species that are best adapted to their environment. He reached these conclusions while studying animal characteristics and developing treatments for animal diseases. Over four hundred years later the nineteenth-century English naturalist Charles Darwin (1809–1882) independently worked out a theory that was similar. He carried his studies far beyond the point where Al-Damiri stopped, developing the theory of evolution.

AN ERROR
ALTERS HISTORY

Islamic scientists were guilty of several major errors in their scientific work. One of these undoubtedly altered history. The ninth-century attempts by astronomers in Al-Ma'mun's House of Wisdom to measure the earth seemed to confirm the figures arrived at by Posidonius of Apamea around 100 B.C. These incorrect figures were passed on down through history instead of Eratosthenes' correct ones.

When Christopher Columbus planned his historic voyage in 1492, he used these incorrect estimates to figure how far west he would have to sail to reach the lands of the East. This and other mistaken information about the size of Asia led Columbus to believe that a voyage of some 2,400 miles (3,800 km) west from

Spain would reach the East Indies. Had he known that the world is 5,000 miles (8,000 km) bigger than he thought it to be, Columbus would never have attempted his great voyage of discovery, because no one believed that ships could sail so far.

Another error of Moslem scientists was that of following Ptolemy's theory that placed the earth at the center of the solar system. Some of the stargazers who followed this theory did begin to sense that something was wrong with it. Al-Biruni's writings show that he accepted the possibility that the sun, not the earth, was the center of the solar system. However, Al-Biruni turned his attention to other fields and never developed a new theory to replace Ptolemy's system.

Thus, instead of discovering the true nature of the solar system, Moslem scientists passed on observational data and half-developed ideas that would be used much later by such European giants as Nicolaus Copernicus, Tycho Brahe, and Johannes Kepler in the fifteenth and sixteenth centuries. Using these data, together with observations of their own, these three men worked out the modern planetary theory that places the sun correctly at the center of the solar system with the planets rotating around it in elliptical orbits.

TWO MAJOR HERITAGES

Moslem scientists passed on to those who followed them two special heritages. One was the preservation of ancient scientific lore developed by the philosophers of Greece, India, Persia, and other civilizations that were crumbling in the seventh century. Many modern scholars question whether the rekindling of the scientific spirit that characterized the Renaissance, and the Age of Enlightenment that followed it, would ever have occurred had the Moslems failed to preserve the ancient lore that they found and collected so carefully.

Nowhere is this process of preservation and development of ancient lore more evident than in mathematics. The Indian numbers that so fascinated Severus Sebokht and Al-Khwarizmi are essential to modern science and civilization.

These "numbers of the Indians," as Al-Khwarizmi called them, traveled west to Spain and spread from there to the rest of Europe. Today everyone around the world, whether schoolchildren, atomic physicists, or stockbrokers, calculates with these symbols that are now called "Arabic numerals."

The second great heritage of Islam was the emphasis it placed on the use of experimental methods. Until the heyday of Islamic scholarship, civilizations had tended to look back and search for answers to scientific questions in the classics of the past. The Moslems collected the wisdom of the ages, but they added large amounts of data gathered through their measurements and careful observations of natural phenomena. Finally, they applied modern scientific methods of analysis, deduction, and experimentation to the ancient lore they inherited from other civilizations.

Such great thinkers as Ibn Sina, Al-Biruni, and Ibn al-Haytham, as well as others who participated in the technological advances of the Moslem world, went far beyond the synthesis of ancient knowledge when they developed entirely new ideas about optics, medicine, mathematics, and geography.

Islamic science thus provided a bridge between the older cultures and the modern world. Like a true bridge, it led in two directions. One gave the present age access to ancient sources of knowledge. The other provided the starting point for a path that has led humankind to the use of experimental methods in order to better understand the nature of the world around us.

GLOSSARY

Alchemy—An ancient quest for knowledge through magical means, including a search for ways to extend life and turn base metals into gold.

Allah—The Arabic name for the Supreme Being.

Astrolabe—An instrument used in medieval times to determine, among other things, the angles of the sun, stars, or planets above the horizon.

Cardial valves—Valves in the circulatory system that open in only one way, keeping the blood flowing in the same direction at all times.

Circa (c.)—About or around; used when an exact date is unknown.

Elixir of life—A magical potion sought by alchemists to extend life or increase youthfulness.

Equinox—The two times of the year (in March and September) when the sun is over the equator and day and night are exactly equal.

Islam—The religion based on the teachings of Mohammed.

Moslem—A person who follows the teachings of Mohammed.

Optics—The study of light and vision.

Renaissance—The period in the fourteenth through sixteenth centuries when a great revival of learning occurred in Europe.

Solstice—The time when the sun is at its greatest distance north (summer solstice) or south (winter solstice) of the equator.

Tourniquet—A bandage bound tightly around an arm or leg to stop the flow of blood in an artery.

Trigonometry—The branch of mathematics dealing with angles and triangles.

Zenith—The highest point in the sky reached by stars or planets.

Zij—The Arabic term for an astronomical table, usually including information on how the calculations were made.

FOR FURTHER READING

Al-Hassan, Ahmad Y., and Hill, Donald R. *Islamic Technology: An Illustrated History*. Cambridge: Cambridge University Press, 1986.

Edmonds, I. G. *Islam*. New York: Franklin Watts, 1977.

Hoyt, Edwin P. *A Short History of Science*. Vol. 1. New York: John Day, 1965.

Ronan, Colin A. *Science: Its History and Development Among the World's Cultures*. New York: Facts On File, 1982.

Ross, Frank, Jr. *Arabs and the Islamic World*. New York: S. G. Phillips, 1979.

Tames, Richard. *The Genius of Arab Civilization*. Cambridge, Mass.: The MIT Press, 1975.

_____. *The Muslim World*. Morristown, N.J.: Silver Burdett, 1982.

INDEX

ABOUT
THE AUTHOR

George Beshore has written about scientific and environmental subjects for newspapers, magazines, and the federal government for over twenty-five years. Now a full-time free-lance writer, he is also the author of *Science in Ancient China*, published by Franklin Watts.